Just For You

TEACHER

Illustrated by

Douglas Hall

A.R.C.A.

Selected by Karen Sullivan

BROCKHAMPTON PRESS

You may give them your love but not your
thoughts.
For they have their own thoughts.
You may house their bodies but not their souls,
For their souls dwell in the house of tomorrow,
which you cannot visit, not even in your dreams.
Kahlil Gibran

I have had playmates, I have had companions,
In my days of childhood, in my joyful school-
days.
Charles Lamb, 'The Old Familiar Faces'

If help and salvation are to come,
they can only come from the children,
for the children are the makers of men.
Maria Montessori

We give you our children — their clean, untouched souls, their eager minds. Nurture them; nourish them. They are our hopes, our future. Can you feel the weight of our trust?

Anonymous, *To a Teacher*

Each child is an adventure into a better life — an opportunity to change the old pattern and make it new.
Hubert H. Humphrey

There is no sinner like a young saint.
Aphra Behn

A teacher is better than two books.
German proverb

. . . a young child, a fresh, uncluttered mind, a world before him — to what treasures will you lead him? With what will you furnish his spirit?
Gladys Hunt

Smartness runs in my family. When I went to school I was so smart my teacher was in my class for five years.
George Burns

I think teachers are nice. They help you if you
have grazed your knee.

Joseph, 5

❖

Thus hand in hand through life we'll go;
Its chequered paths of joy and woe
With cautious steps we'll tread.

Nathaniel Cotton

❖

You can't expect a boy to be vicious till he's been
to a good school.

Saki

❖

To teach is to learn twice over.

Confucius

There is a tomorrow coming by and by when the lisper of the ABC will be the master of a home of his own . . . .

Cuyler

Life is indeed darkness save when there is urge,
And all urge is blind save when there is knowledge,
And all knowledge is vain save when there is work,
And all work is empty save when there is love.

Kahlil Gibran

Teaching has ruined more American novelists than drink.

Gore Vidal

Lord, make me a channel of thy peace . . . .
That where there is despair I may bring hope.
St Francis of Assisi

My teacher is good to me.
Hannah, 5

If a man keeps cherishing his old knowledge
so as continually to be acquiring new, he may
be a teacher of others.
Confucius

To be good is noble, but to teach others how to be good is nobler — and no trouble.
Mark Twain

You are the bows from which your children as living arrows are sent forth.
Kahlil Gibran

But Eeyore was saying to himself: 'This writing business. Pencils and what-not. Over-rated, if you ask me. Silly stuff. Nothing in it.'
A. A. Milne, *Winnie-the-Pooh*

How, after six years of complete attention, complete trust, can my child have been converted in just one day to the unquestionable rightness of the teacher?
Sarah Bane

Foolishness is bound in the heart of a child; but the rod of correction shall drive it far from him.
The Torah

No man can tell but he that loves his children, how many delicious accents make a man's heart dance in the pretty conversation of those dear pledges; their childishness, their stammering, their little angers, their innocence, their imperfections, their necessities, are so many little emanations of joy and comfort to him that delights in their persons and society.

Jeremy Taylor

Here lie Willie Michie's banes;
O Satan, when ye tak him,
Gie him the schoolin of your weans,
For clever deils he'll mak them!

Robert Burns, 'Epitaph on a Schoolmaster'

A teacher stands in fear of teaching.

French proverb

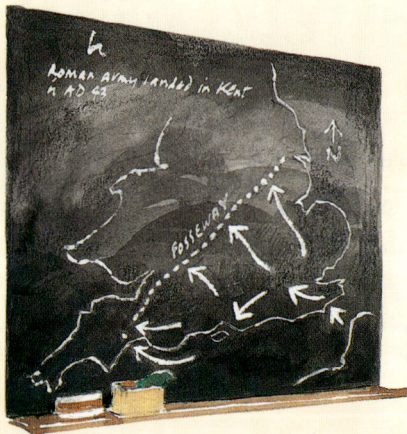

He teacheth ill,
who teacheth all.

English proverb

The schoolmaster is abroad, and I trust more to him, armed with his primer, than I do to the soldier in full military array, for upholding and extending the liberties of his country.

Lord Brougham, speech in the House of Commons, 1828

Education is what survives when what has been learned has been forgotten.

B. F. Skinner

In the 1880s, a Dr Heath at Eton College created what may be a record by whipping seventy boys, one after another. He injured himself so badly that he was laid up with aches and pains for more than a week.

Plant the seeds
Watch them grow
Package them up
And off they go.
Kitty Browne

Naturally I tried to give the boys some seri-
ous teaching, and soon found that very little
actual sitting down to it was required. At
least on my part.
Molly Hughes, *A Victorian Family*

How am I to sing your praise,
Happy chimney-corner days,
Sitting safe in nursery nooks,
Reading picture story-books?
Robert Louis Stevenson

Whom God teaches, man cannot.

Japanese proverb

Education is an admirable thing, but it is well
to remember from time to time that nothing that
is worth knowing can be taught.

Oscar Wilde

He is a teacher, showing me how to look at
things anew.

Arnold Zable, 'My First Love'

Finish every day and be done with it.
You have done what you could.
Ralph Waldo Emerson

◈

Learning. The kind of ignorance distinguishing
the studious.
Ambrose Bierce

◈

Sitting beside him on the board laid across the
bobsled, Laura did not say anything either.
There was nothing to say. She was on her way
to teach school. Only yesterday she was a
schoolgirl; now she was a school-teacher. This
had happened so suddenly . . . .
Laura Ingalls Wilder, *These Happy Golden Years*

INTEGRATING FACTOR

E.G.: if the differential equation

$$\frac{dy}{x} + \frac{y}{x^2}\,dx = 0$$

is multiplied by x^2, there results

$$x\,dy + y\,dx = 0,$$

which has the solution $xy = C$.

The differential equation

$$xy'' + (3 - x^3)y' - 5x^2 y + 4x = 0$$

has the integrating factor x^2;
when multiplied by x^2 the
equation becomes

$$\frac{d}{dx}\left(x^3 y' - x^5 y + x^4\right) = 0.$$

Listening to Miss Anthony,
our lovely Miss,
Charming us dumb with
The Wind in the Willows.

D. J. Enright, 'Two Good Things...'

It is safer to learn than to teach; and who conceals
his opinion has nothing to answer for.
William Penn

A little learning is a dangerous thing.
Spanish proverb

Dancing Sellinger's Round, and dancing and
Dancing it, and getting it perfect forever.
D. J. Enright, 'Two Good Things in Primary School'

In the information age, you don't teach philosophy
as they did after feudalism. You perform it. If
Aristotle were alive today he'd have a talk show.
Timothy Leary

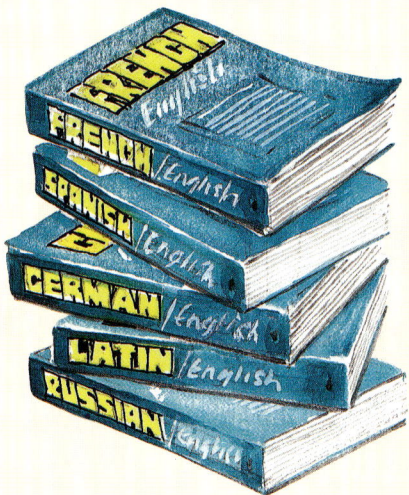

Knowledge, teaching and words may be deeds.

Spanish proverb

Teachers can be nice to help you.

Scarlett, 6

Education is a companion which no misfortune can depress, no crime can destroy, no enemy can alienate, no despotism can enslave. At home a friend, abroad an introduction, in solitude a solace, and in society an ornament. It chastens vice, it guides virtue, it gives, at once, grace and government to genius. Without it, what is man? A splendid slave, a reasoning savage.

Joseph Addison

There are no national frontiers to learning.

Japanese proverb

Everybody who is incapable of learning has taken to teaching.
Oscar Wilde

I expect you'll be becoming a schoolmaster, sir. That's what most of the gentlemen does, sir, that gets sent down for indecent behaviour.
Evelyn Waugh, *Decline and Fall*

Facts were never pleasing to him. He acquired them with reluctance and got rid of them with relief. He was never on terms with them until he had stood them on their heads.
J. M. Barrie

A teacher affects eternity; he can never tell where his influence stops.

Henry B. Adams, *The Education of Henry Adams*

A teacher should have maxi-
mal authority and mini-
mal power.

Thomas Szasz, *The Second Sin*

For rigorous teachers seized my youth,
And purged its faith, and trimmed its fire,
Showed me the high, white star of Truth,
There bade me gaze, and there aspire.

Matthew Arnold, 'Stanzas from the Grande Chartreuse'

Horse-play,
romping, frequent
and loud fits of laughter,
jokes, waggery, and indiscriminate
familiarity, will sink both merit and knowledge into a degree of contempt. They compose at
most a merry fellow; and a merry fellow was never
yet a respectable man.
Lord Chesterfield

Prejudices, it is well known, are most difficult to
eradicate from the heart whose soil has never been
loosened or fertilized by education; they grow
there, firm as weeds among stones.

Charlotte Brontë, *Jane Eyre*

Now what I want is, Facts. Teach these boys and girls nothing but Facts. Facts alone are wanted in life. Plant nothing else, and root out everything else . . . . Stick to Facts, sir!

Charles Dickens, *Hard Times*

Learning without thought is labour lost; thought without learning is perilous.

Confucius

Ignorance
is a right!
Education is
eroding one of
the few democratic freedoms
remaining to us!

Christopher Andreae

A man who has never gone to school may steal from a freight car, but if he has a university education, he may steal the whole railroad.
Franklin D. Roosevelt

Education is the ability to listen to almost anything without losing your temper or your self-confidence.
Robert Frost

He who can, does. He who cannot, teaches.
George Bernard Shaw, *Man and Superman*

We schoolmasters must temper discretion with deceit.
Evelyn Waugh

There's Pooh, he thought to himself. Pooh hasn't much Brain, but he never comes to any harm. He does silly things and they turn out right. There's Owl. Owl hasn't exactly got Brain, but he Knows Things. He would know the Right Thing to Do when Surrounded by Water. There's Rabbit. He hasn't Learnt in Books, but he can always Think of a Clever Plan. There's Kanga. She isn't Clever, Kanga isn't, but she would be so anxious about Roo that she would do a Good Thing to Do without thinking about it . . . .

A. A. Milne, *Winnie-the-Pooh*

Teachers give you hard work.

Emily, 5

Give me a girl at an impressionable age, and
she is mine for life!
Muriel Spark, *The Prime of Miss Jean Brodie*

No bubble is so iridescent or floats longer than
that blown by the successful teacher.
Sir William Osler

What office is there which involves more
responsibility, which requires more qualifica-
tions, and which ought, therefore, to be more
honourable, than that of teaching?
Harriet Martineau

Education doesn't change life much. It just lifts trouble to a higher plane of regard.

Robert Frost

Now, if the principle of toleration were once admitted into classical education — if it were admitted that the great object is to read and enjoy a language, and the stress of the teaching were placed on the few things absolutely essential to this result, if the tortoise were allowed time to creep, and the bird permitted to fly, and the fish to swim, towards the enchanted and divine sources of Helicon — all might in their own way arrive there, and rejoice in its flowers, its beauty, and its coolness.

Harriet Beecher Stowe

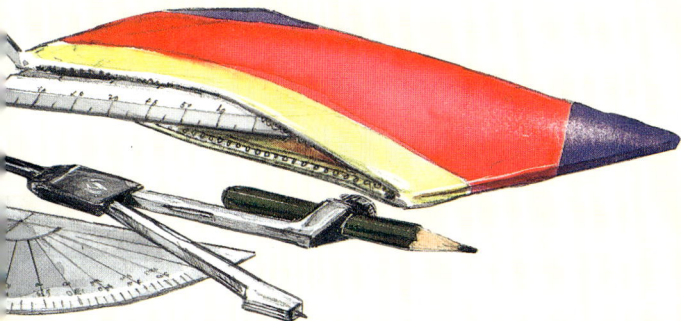

There is no crisis to which academics will not respond with a seminar.

Marvin Bressler

One looks back with appreciation to the brilliant teachers, but with gratitude to those who touched our human feelings. The curriculum is so much necessary raw material, but warmth is the vital element for the growing plant and for the soul of the child.

Carl Jung

Education is when you read the fine print.
Experience is what you get if you don't.

Pete Seeger

Well had the boding tremblers
learned to trace
The day's disasters in his morning face.

Oliver Goldsmith

Teachers are kind.

Cate, 5

It is the supreme art of the teacher to awaken joy in creative expression and knowledge.
Albert Einstein

Housework is a breeze. Cooking is a pleasant diversion. Putting up a retaining wall is a lark. But teaching is like climbing a mountain.
Fawn M. Brodie

Teachers can be cross. They can be kind. They can help.
Max, 5

Life is amazing: and the teacher had better pre-
pare himself to be a medium for that amazement.
Edward Blishen

A schoolmaster should have an atmosphere of awe,
and walk wonderingly, as if he was amazed at
being himself.
Walter Bagehot

To know how to suggest is the great art of teaching. To attain it we must be able to guess what
will interest; we must learn to read the childish
soul as we might a piece of music. Then, by simply
changing the key, we keep up the attraction and
vary the song.
Henri-Frédéric Amiel

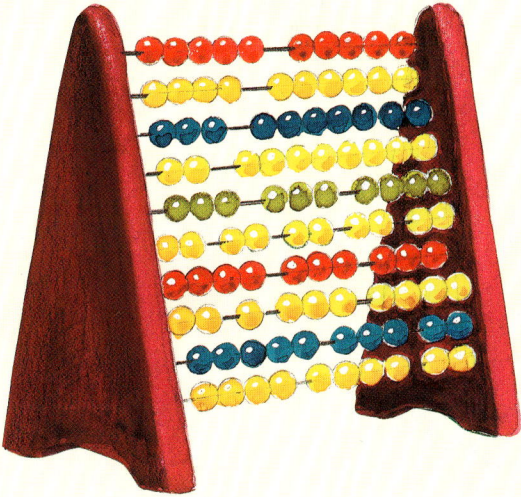

I swear . . . to hold my teacher in this art equal to my own parents; to make him partner in my livelihood; when he is in need of money to share mine with him; to consider his family as my own brothers and to teach them this art, if they want to learn it, without fee or indenture.

Hippocrates

No one can look back on his schooldays and say
with truth that they were altogether unhappy.
George Orwell

My dear dear Mother,
If you don't let me come home I die — I am all
over ink, and my fine clothes have been spoilt —
I have been
tost in a blanket,
and seen a ghost.
I remain, my dear dear Mother,
Your dutiful and most unhappy son,
Freddy.
P.S. Remember me to my Father.
Frederick Reynolds, letter written home on his second day of
school, 1775

And gladly would he learn, and gladly teach.
Chaucer, *The Canterbury Tales*

Who dares to teach must never cease to learn.
John Cotton Dana

The whole art of teaching is only the art of awakening the natural curiosity of young minds for the purpose of satisfying it afterwards.
Anatole France

Men must be taught as if
you taught them not,
And things proposed as
things forgot.
Alexander Pope

Nothing in education
is so astonishing as
the amount of igno-
rance it accumulates
in the form of inert
facts.
Henry B. Adams,
*The Education
of Henry
Adams*

The roots of education are bitter, but the fruit is sweet.
Aristotle

The test and the use of man's education is that
he finds pleasure in the exercise of his mind.
Jacques Barzun

I'm for bringing back the birch, but only
for consenting adults.

Gore Vidal

Teachers make hard work and love you.
And get cross.

William, 5

'Reeling and Writhing, of course, to begin with,'
the Mock Turtle replied, 'and then the different
branches of Arithmetic — Ambition, Distraction,
Uglification, and Derision.'

Lewis Carroll, *Alice's Adventures in Wonderland*

University politics are vicious precisely because the stakes are so small.
Henry Kissinger

The purpose of education is to replace an empty mind with a full one.
Malcolm Forbes

The office of the scholar is to cheer, to raise, and to guide men by showing them facts amidst appearances. He plies the slow, unhonoured, and unpaid task of observation. . . . He is the world's eye.
Ralph Waldo Emerson

The learner always begins by
finding fault, but the scholar sees the positive
merit in everything.

Georg Hegel

If you think education is expensive, try ignorance.

Derek Bok

At school, friendship is a passion. It entrances the being; it tears the soul. All loves of afterlife can never bring its rapture, or its wretchedness; no bliss so absorbing, no pangs of jealousy or despair so crushing and so keen! What tenderness and what devotion; what illimitable confidence, infinite revelations of inmost thoughts; what ecstatic present and romantic future; what bitter estrangements and what melting reconciliations . . . what earthquakes of the heart and whirlwinds of the soul are confined in that simple phrase, a schoolboy's friendship!

Benjamin Disraeli, *Coningsby*

Permissiveness is the principle of treating children as if they were adults; and the tactic of making sure they never reach that stage.

Thomas Szasz

People commonly educate their children as they build their houses, according to some plan they think beautiful, without considering whether it is suited to the purposes for which they are designed.

Lady Mary Wortley Montagu

Never seem wiser, nor more learned, than the people you are with. Wear your learning, like your watch, in a private pocket: and do not merely pull it out and strike it, merely to show that you have one.

Lord Chesterfield

The professors laugh at themselves, they laugh at life; they long ago abjured the bitch-goddess Success, and the best of them will fight for his scholastic ideals with a courage and persistence that would shame a soldier. The professor is not afraid of words like truth; in fact he is not afraid of words at all.

Catherine Drinker Bowen

Teaching is not a lost art, but the regard for it is a lost tradition.

Jacques Barzun

Erudition. Dust shaken out of a book into an empty skull.

Ambrose Bierce

It is by teaching that we teach ourselves, by relating that we observe, by affirming that we examine, by showing that we look, by writing that we think, by pumping that we draw water into the well.

Henri-Frédéric Amiel

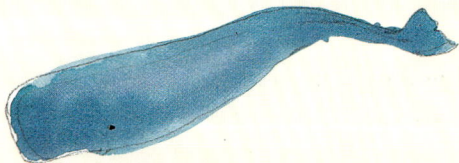

If the past cannot teach the present and the father cannot teach the son, then history need not have bothered to go on, and the world has wasted a great deal of time.
Russell Hoban

❖

The most important part of teaching —
to teach what it is to know.
Simone Weil

❖

Education is the process of casting false pearls before real swine.
Irwin Edman

The mind of Man is framed even like the breath
And harmony of music. There is a dark
Invisible workmanship that reconciles
Discordant elements and makes them move
In one society. Ah me! that all
The terrors, all the early miseries,
Regrets, vexations, lassitudes, that all
The thoughts and feelings which have been
infused
into my mind, should ever have made up
The calm existence that is mine when I
Am worthy of myself . . . .

William Wordsworth, *The Prelude*

Discipline is a symbol of caring to a child.
He needs guidance. If there is love, there is
no such thing as being too tough with a child.
Bette Davis

53

'That's the way to tackle things,' said Pa. 'Have confidence in yourself, and you can lick anything. You have·confidence in yourself, and that's the only way to make other folks have confidence in you.'

Laura Ingalls Wilder, *These Happy Golden Years*

Our attitude towards ourselves should be 'to be satiable in learning' and towards others 'to be tireless in teaching.'

Mao Zedong

There is nothing can pay one for that invaluable ignorance which is the companion of youth, those sanguine groundless hopes, and that lively vanity which makes all the happiness of life.

Lady Mary Wortley Montagu

The exquisite art of idleness, one of the most important things that any University can teach.
Oscar Wilde

In a time of drastic change it is the learners who inherit the future. The learned usually find themselves equipped to live in a world that no longer exists.
Eric Hoffer

He who wishes to teach us a truth should not tell it to us, but simply suggest it with a brief gesture, a gesture which starts an ideal trajectory in the air along which we glide until we find ourselves at the feet of the new truth.
José Ortega y Gasset, *The Revolt of the Masses*

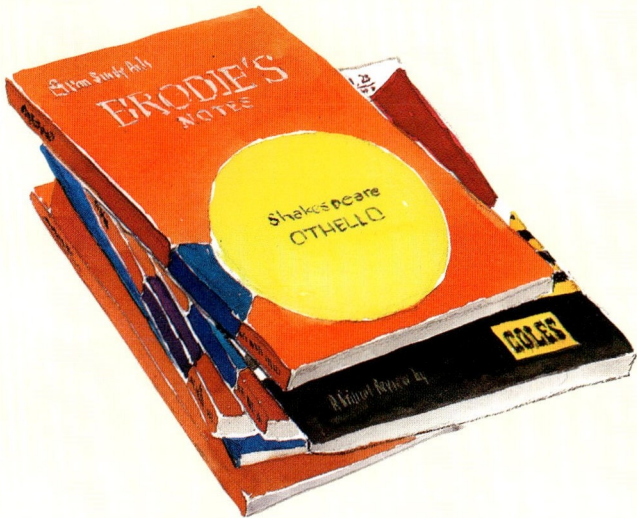

Spoon feeding in the long run teaches us nothing but the shape of the spoon.

E. M. Forster

Good teaching is one-fourth preparation and three-fourths theatre.

Gail Godwin

How can you dare
teach a man to read
until you've taught
him everything else
first?

George Bernard Shaw

Ignorance . . . is a painless evil; so, I should think,
is dirt, considering the merry faces that go along
with it.
George Eliot

You must teach children that the ground beneath
their feet is the ashes of your grandfathers. So that
they will respect the land, tell children that the
earth is rich with the lives of our kin. Teach children what we have taught our children, that the
earth is our mother. Whatever befalls the earth
befalls the sons of the earth. If men spit upon the
ground, they spit upon themselves.
Seattle, Chief of the Duwamish, Suquamish
and allied Indian tribes

Even a minor event in the life of a child is an event of that child's world and thus a world event.

Gaston Bachelard

Acknowledgements:

The Publishers wish to thank everyone who gave permission to reproduce the quotes in this book. Every effort has been made to contact the copyright holders, but in the event that an oversight has occurred, the publishers would be delighted to rectify any omissions in future editions of this book. Children's quotes printed courtesy of Herne Hill School; D. J. Enright, extract from *Two Good Things in Primary School,* from *The Terrible Shears,* reprinted courtesy of Chatto & Windus; Evelyn Waugh, reprinted courtesy of Hulton Management and Peters, Fraser and Dunlop; A. A. Milne, reprinted courtesy of Methuen Children's Books and Curtis Brown Limited, London, copyright by E. P. Dutton, renewed by A. A. Milne; George Bernard Shaw reprinted courtesy of the Society of Authors on behalf of the Estate of George Bernard Shaw; Robert Frost from *The Poetry of Robert Frost,* reprinted by permission of Jonathan Cape, the Estate of Robert Frost and Peter A. Gilbert, North Hampshire, USA © Robert Frost; *The Huge Joke Book* edited by Kevin Goldstein-Jackson, Ernest Ford and A. C. H. Newman, Elliott Right Way Books © A. C. H. Newman, Ernest Ford and Elliott Right Way Books; Laura Ingalls Wilder © Laura Ingalls Wilder, 1932, reprinted courtesy of Methuen Children's Books.